Then & Now

Workington

Then & Now
Workington

Richard L.M. Byers

TEMPUS

Frontispiece: The 25 August 2006 is a date etched into
the industrial history of Workington forever, for it
was the day that the last ever steel railway line was
produced at the Moss Bay works, signalling the end of
a long tradition of iron and steel manufacture extending back to the mid-eighteenth century. This unique
photograph shows the two sections of the final steel
rail rolled that day. It was taken just moments after
they had emerged onto the rail bank at just before 3.00
p.m., and signalling the end of 129 years and 12 days
of steel rail manufacture in Workington. Production at
the United Kingdom's oldest and only rail producer had
ceased forever.

First published 2006

Tempus Publishing Limited
The Mill, Brimscombe Port,
Stroud, Gloucestershire, GL5 2QG
www.tempus-publishing.com

© Richard L.M. Byers, 2006

The right of Richard L.M. Byers to be identified as the Author
of this work has been asserted in accordance with the
Copyrights, Designs and Patents Act 1988.

All rights reserved. No part of this book may be reprinted
or reproduced or utilised in any form or by any electronic,
mechanical or other means, now known or hereafter invented,
including photocopying and recording, or in any information
storage or retrieval system, without the permission in writing
from the Publishers.

British Library Cataloguing in Publication Data.
A catalogue record for this book is available from the British Library.

ISBN 0 7524 3744 5

Series design and typesetting by Liz Rudderham.
Origination by Tempus Publishing Limited.
Printed in Great Britain.

Contents

Tempus Fugit - time flies. On 1 July 2006, Workington's new £200,000 interactive clock, called Lookout, designed by Andy Plant and Matt Wand was unveiled. A fitting reminder that time is continuous, something that we can measure but not control. Time inevitably brings change and the Workington townscape has seen more than its fair share of often radical change. Many of the places and buildings depicted in this book have suffered the ravages of time, few have really survived. Perhaps, the new clock within the town centre is also a symbol of a new beginning, a new era. Only time will tell and that's assuming the controversial clock itself stands the test of time.

Acknowledgements

The author wishes to acknowledge with grateful thanks the assistance and contributions offered by Jo E. Byers, Joyce Byers, Michael Burridge, Phil Croach (Helena Thompson Museum), Janet Thompson, Rebecca Walker (Marks & Spencer), Colin Sharpe (Port of Workington), John and Erica Irlam, Janet Thompson, Carol Gray (Workington Town Centre manager) and Steve White (Carlisle Library). Permission to reproduce the archive photographs on the following pages was kindly granted by Marks & Spencers Archives (pages 14 and 15), Helena Thompson Museum (pages 24, 70 and 71) and Carlisle Library (pages 38, 40 and 75).

Introduction

I have often said that researching the past can be likened to attempting a massive jigsaw puzzle. But it is not as simple as turning all the pieces the right way up and separating the straight edges from the squiggly ones. History is irregularly shaped, not everything fits together and the jigsaw is virtually always complicated by several missing pieces. Having previously written about and recorded so much of Workington's history, many people seem to think that I know everything there is to know about the town's past. But in reality this is far from the truth. Barely a week goes by without me discovering something new I had previously never been aware of. Often this is simply some small, almost forgotten fragment of information which helps add another piece to the big jigsaw. Sometimes it is an old and rare photograph that has lain unseen for many generations.

My task in compiling this book is to bring together many of these previously unpublished images with others from my collection, and to compare them with modern ones taken from exactly the same locations. By adding accompanying text to each pair, the reader can follow and reflect on the many changes that have occurred over the last hundred years or so, and then revisit the locations to see them in a new light, just as they were by earlier generations of Workingtonians.

Step back in time to when there was a roof on Workington Hall and steam trains trundled through the centre of the town, their sooty smoke billowing up into Pow Street. The town had five cinemas and you could see a different film every night of the week. The sweet smell of brewing from the John Peel brewery hung in the air, pedestrians ruled the streets and the sight of a motor car was a rarity. Do you remember when our streets were filled with small independent shops, stretching from Washington Street and Wilson Street, down Pow Street and Finkle Street, all the way down Fisher Street and Station Road? The majority of these sadly disappeared as the town's shopping precinct was built in the late 1960s and early '70s. Along with buildings such as Central Station, the Drill Hall and St Johns School which once proudly occupied the site. This school was responsible for educating many generations of the town's children and the sound of them laughing and playing in the school yard often spilled over into Pow Street and beyond.

Remarkably as I am completing this book the town centre is undergoing yet another major redevelopment. Large blocks of property which were barely thirty years old have themselves been demolished. Will the lessons learnt from the previous quite unsympathetic development ensure that this new town centre will serve Workington significantly longer? Only time will tell and by then how much more will the townscape have changed. I hope this book along with my others will go someway to raise a greater awareness and foster a lasting appreciation of the town, and in particular celebrate its past. There is an awful lot yet to discover out there, young or old, our local history still has the power to amaze, delight and excite us. As for my jigsaw, I doubt if I will ever finish it.

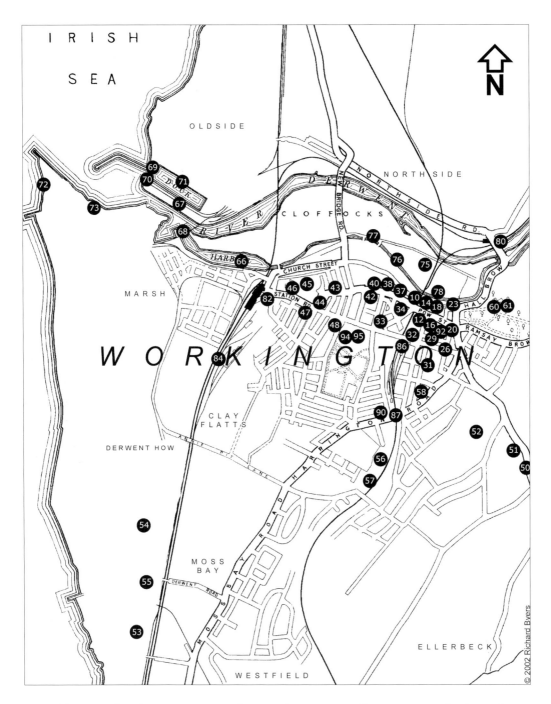

Map of the town of Workington, *c.* 1950. At this time the town was still a major centre for the production of iron and steel, employing thousands of people, Solway Pit had only recently been sunk and the harbour was a bustling and busy port, visited by many hundreds of ships each year. The majority of buildings and sites mentioned in this book are identified on this map by their relevant page number.

Town Centre

*L*ooking down to the foot of Ramsey Brow, *c.* 1919. During the last half century the town centre of Workington has undergone significant and radical changes, not just in respect of its main shopping streets, but also the road system that surrounds it. The town grew rapidly in Victorian times, long before the advent of the motor car and with little thought of town planning. No one could have envisaged the thousands of vehicles using the town's roads today. This post First World War photograph records just how narrow Ramsey Brow once was, probably barely 3 metres wide. This obvious bottleneck was not isolated to this junction. All the older properties on the west side of Washington Street and Bridge Street, from St Johns church through to the top of Hall Brow have been demolished to provide wider roads. Pow Street, which once extended across the end of Washington Street, has also been significantly shortened. An extensive new road system, extending to several lanes in places and controlled by five sets of traffic lights, now eases traffic through this area.

*T*he east corner of Pow Street and Speedwell Lane, *c.* 1949 and 2005. This side of Pow Street was once dominated by the imposing and elegant Victorian façade of the Clydesdale and North of Scotland Bank, now known simply as the Clydesdale Bank. Opened during the early 1880s, the three-storey bank premises were actually built over the Cleator & Workington Junction Railway line which ran in a cutting below the street level. This length of track carried trains from Workington Central Station, over Navvies Bridge to Siddick Junction and up to Seaton, as well as down to Workington Bridge Station at the foot of Calva Brow, on the north side of the River Derwent. Originally only a quite narrow stone bridge linked this end of Pow Street with Finkle Street and spanned the railway line below. Today, this part of the street is particularly wide and has now been landscaped and pedestrianized. Beneath your feet the old railway line is now the service road linking Central Square with the Cloffolks car park. (see page 81)

A nother look at the east corner of Pow Street and Speedwell Lane in 1971 and 2005. The lovely old Victorian Clydesdale Bank premises shown on the previous page were replaced by the present modern building in the early 1960s and have really changed little in the last forty or so years. Beside the new bank was opened Liptons, the town's first supermarket. Today, Liptons would be considered very small by comparison with Workington's present larger out of town food stores, located on the Cloffolks and Derwent How, but at the time it was a revelation for the town. Previously no other grocer's shop was self service, where customers filled their own baskets. The Lipton supermarket was eventually closed after the company was taken over by Presto, who later became part of Safeways and ultimately Morrisons. The premises were acquired by the Halifax Building Society, who later became the Halifax Bank.

*L*ooking south towards Murray Road from the end of Pow Street, *c.* 1962 and 2005. The older photograph shows part of the substantial sandstone parapet wall of the railway bridge that linked this end of Pow Street with Finkle Street, directly opposite the Clydesdale Bank. Opened in 1878, the Cleator & Workington Junction Railway Co., which operated the line, was predominantly a mineral railway and hauled coal, iron ore, limestone and railway lines between the local pits, iron and steelworks and the harbour. Until 1923, when the company was absorbed into the London Midland Scottish, the passenger services on the line were operated by the Furness Railway. Often this part of the street was filled with sooty smoke and steam from the boilers of the trains which passed back and forth below the bridge. In the centre of the photograph we can see the rear of the Ritz Cinema over the parapet wall of the bridge. To the right of the photograph we can see the old post office building on the corner of Murray Road and Finkle Street.

*L*ooking east down Pow Street from the end of Finkle Street, *c.* 1949 and 2005. On the extreme left of the photograph is the Woolworth's store first opened here in 1930, beside which are the original premises of Marks & Spencer, where the present Iceland food store is located. Woolworths once boasted that everything they sold cost just 3d or 6d. Directly opposite as Pow Street narrowed was Joseph Goss' grocers shop. Unlike the Lipton's supermarket which opened on the other side of the street during the 1960s, Goss' was a traditional old grocer's shop where all customers queued behind a large wooden counter to be served. The assistants would then personally assemble and pack your order, rushing back and forth weighing and packing foodstuffs to your individual requirements. Larger orders could be delivered by a boy on a bicycle.

Nos 62 to 64 Pow Street 1936 and 2006. The earlier photograph provides a valuable record of this prominent site, prior to the construction of the first Marks & Spencer store. Opened on 10 July 1936 the new M&S, with its once trademark neat redbrick and stone façade, occupied only the site of Nicholson's butchers shop, extending to the right of the photograph across the narrow cobbled lane. Out of the picture, Melias' grocers shop was located on the other side of this lane, in the property today occupied by the Bradford & Bingley Building Society. The delivery boy's bicycle with its square, wicker basket, is leaning against the wall. The very narrow shop to the left stood for a further

twenty-two years or so. Eventually it too was acquired by M&S and the little shop, which at one time was occupied by Boots the Chemist, was demolished and M&S extended once more in 1959. Today, the Iceland food store occupies the site, Marks & Spencer having moved further east along Pow Street.

*T*he west end of Pow Street, looking towards Finkle Street from the end of Tiffin Lane, *c.* 1960 and 2006. Following on from the previous page we can see the extended Marks & Spencer's store in the centre of the earlier photograph. Ajoining M&S is the original frontage of the Woolworths store, seen previously on page 10. Both these properties have today been replaced with much larger modern buildings. Melias' grocers shop, with its sunblind extended over the shop window, can also be clearly seen. The block of property on the extreme left of the picture, which included WH Smiths, Timpsons shoes shop, the Grapes Inn public house and Goss' grocers shop (see page 13) was demolished during the late 1960s to make way for St John's Shopping Precinct. The Grapes had

been in existence since at least the mid-nineteenth century, and up until the 1950s still had a number of stables and a hayloft at the rear, a legacy from the days before the motor car when many people travelled on horseback or in a pony and trap. There were once two other public houses in the town with the same name, one in Brow Top and the other in King Street. The latter still survives today.

*L*ooking north down Ivison Lane towards Pow Street in May 2005 and July 2006. The street plan of Workington's town centre has changed several times in the last forty or so years. Originally at this point Pow Street met John Street. Then the latter extended from Central Square through to this junction. With the first redevelopment of the town centre in the late 1960s, this length of John Street disappeared and the street became St John's shopping precinct. It is now Ivison Lane, named in honour of the former Workington Town rugby league player Bill Ivison. The later photograph shows the impressive new interactive clock which has a minute hand that revolves horizontally in a circle above a spherical, stainless steel base. At the end of the minute hand a camera points down to numerals of the clock face in the paving area below. The hour is indicated in a collar just below the minute hand. Peep holes are located at different levels around the globe to view the camera images. On the hour, the minute hand rises and points vertically to the sky and panoramic views across the town centre are displayed in these windows. On the half hour, music and dialect recordings are heard from speakers surrounding the clock. The clock was unveiled on Saturday 1 July 2006 by Allerdale's Mayor Joe Mumberson and cost around £200,000.

*L*ooking east up Pow Street from the end of Tiffin Lane, *c.* 1910 and 2005. The entrance to the Opera House shown on the previous page can be seen to the left of the older photograph. Today the site is occupied by the Card Warehouse but the property was originally built for Montague Burtons the tailors which opened in February 1929, apparently a smaller replica of Burton's premises in the Strand. The front elevation boasted uninterrupted plate glass windows along its 15 metre frontage and was then the largest shop window in the town. The upper part of the elevation is finished in white 'ceramo' glazed terracotta tiles. The theatre was located to the rear of Burtons and became known as the New Opera House, playing host to a number of famous variety acts including Morecambe and Wise, Frankie Howard and Norman Wisdom. In 1963, the building was converted into the Opera Bingo and Social Club.

*N*os 26 and 28 Pow Street viewed from the car park where the Savings Bank once stood in 1971 and 2005. Over the years the elegant block of shops which once occupied the site have been home to a variety of businesses, including Smallwood's furnishers and Ross Mitchells. Adjoining these properties, to the left in the older photograph, was the District Bank which started life as the Bank of Whitehaven in 1837. It was later acquired by the Manchester and Liverpool District Bank in 1916, and around eight years later its name was shortened to the District Bank. In the 1960s the bank was amalgamated into the National Westminster Bank. At this time they also had two other branches in the town, one on Murray Road (now the Cumberland Building Society) and their existing branch just a short distance away on the corner of Pow Street and John Street (now Ivison Lane). The later photograph shows much of the site is now occupied by Marks & Spencer's (opened in August 1992) and extends through to Udale Street.

The north side of Pow Street, looking west from the corner of Sanderson Street in 1971 and 2006. This row of relatively small shops is again indicative of the type of properties that once existed along the main shopping streets in the town before the arrival of the large national stores. The Maypole shop in the centre of the older photograph was one of three or four grocer's shops in the space of just a few hundred yards. No longer does the housewife walk into town with her basket every day or so to shop at her favourite grocer's shop. The Maypole and Radio Rentals premises are now occupied by the Superfish fish and chip restaurant, opened during the late 1980s by the Herbert family. An earlier generation of the same family ran the Milk Bar in Murray Road. The older photograph shows how narrow Pow Street was at this point. It was a one way street, but parked cars and delivery vehicles could bring the traffic to a standstill.

*L*ooking west along Pow Street from its junction with Washington Street, *c.* 1910 and 2005. The corner of Udale Street can be seen almost in the centre of the picture on the right hand side of the road. At this end of Pow Street, the only remaining building is the former Cumberland Union Bank, later acquired by the Midland Bank, now HSBC. This is just out of view and adjoined Hattersley's shoe shop to the left of the older photograph. The massive façade of the recently completed Debenhams store now dominates the south side of the street. At this point, Sanderson Street once emerged onto Pow Street, directly opposite Udale Street. Thompson Street has also disappeared from the town's street map under the store. The

properties opposite the HSBC bank, including those houses on the west side of Bridge Street and the east side of Udale Street, have been replaced by a car park.

*T*he junction of Washington Street and Pow Street, looking west down Pow Street from the foot of Wilson Street and Ramsey Brow. A good point of reference in the earlier picture is a gas lamp on the left hand side of the street seen again on the opposite page in the foreground, outside Hattersley's shoe shop. Unlike today, the properties on the north side of Pow Street extended across the end of Washington Street. In order to reach Hall Brow, vehicles passing along Washington Street had to make a very tight right turn and then a sharp left into Bridge Street. Over the years a number of road improvements have been carried out here, including the demolition of a section of Pow Street in order that Washington Street be connected directly through to Bridge Street. The Lowther Arms on the left and Hattersley's shoe shop were both removed to further widen the street.

*L*ooking north from the lower part of Wilson Street, across the foot of Ramsey Brow and along Bridge Street, *c.* 1912 and 2005. All the houses on Bridge Street have been cleared, together with the large block of property projecting into Wilson Street on the left of the older photograph – removed to widen the street. Today, Wilson Street leads a nocturnal existence, only coming to life in the evening as its pubs and bars open. Less than forty years ago it was a thriving shopping street with numerous little shops, including James Ellwood's saddlers shop at No. 22. Jimmy served an apprenticeship with his father, who in turn had learnt the art of cutting, sewing and shaping leather from his father. These three generations of the family are particularly famous for making the balls for the town's annual Uppies and Downies contests.

*L*ooking south towards the corner of Bridge Street and Udale Street, *c.* 1973 and 2005. This route in and out of the town follows the old turnpike road north to Maryport. Crossing the River Derwent via Workington Bridge, it then ran along Northside Road before turning north and following what is now the A596. The older photograph, taken just days before these properties were demolished, records just how narrow the street was at this point. It is now an extremely busy thoroughfare. While we mourn the loss of older properties such as these in Bridge Street the advantages of smoothly flowing traffic sometimes wins over the architectural merits of sub-standard properties that have to be removed. The Globe Inn in the centre of the earlier photograph is said to have existed on this site since the early nineteenth century when its landlord was William Iredale. It was later acquired by the Workington Brewery Co. whose brewery was just across the street in Ladies Walk.

*T*he Old Market Place looking north from the foot of King Street, c. 1912 and 2005. The town's Market Charter was granted by Queen Elizabeth I in 1573, and over the years has been held in several locations around the town. This area at the intersection of Nook Street, Curwen Street and King Street (formally General Street) was one of the earliest. It was known as 'Old Market Place' well over a hundred and fifty years ago. After the covered market was built in Portland Street in 1860, the weekly Butter Market continued to be held here. Women from the surrounding villages would walk into town and sell their butter and eggs in this area from large baskets. Markets in the town were originally controlled by the Curwen family, as lords of the manor, but in 1890 the market rights passed to the Local Authority. An interesting feature of the earlier photograph is the large block extending into Market Place, behind the horse and cart to the left. This was the former Carlisle City and District Bank, which was demolished in 1916.

*T*he former Workington Brewery warehouses in Upper Jane Street, *c.* 1975 and 2005. Workington Brewery Company was formed in 1891 by the Iredale family, who had operated in Ladies Walk at the top of Hall Brow since 1839. Their extensive warehouses in Upper Jane Street extended through to the top of Wilson Street and used to store wines and spirits when the company held one of the most comprehensive stocks in the North.

It was once a common sight to see their distinctive red lorries on this side of the street, loading and unloading casks and crates. This often led to congestion of the narrow street. After the brewery was sold, the warehouses were acquired by the Chambers family and over the years have been occupied by a variety of businesses. During the 1980s they were converted into a restaurant, fitness studio, print shop and offices. Today, much of the property is occupied by solicitors Kevin J. Commons & Co.

*L*ooking west down Jane Street across its junction with Washington Street from the foot of Upper Jane Street, *c.* 1935 and 2005. Very little of the property which once existed around this now busy junction still remains. This view was once dominated by the Old Crown Hotel in the centre of the photograph and the New Crown Hotel on the opposite corner. The latter was demolished in the 1970s and stood on the site of the present Washington Central Hotel. The Old Crown was purchased by the local authority in 1937 and later demolished to widen and improve the junction. The Old Crown was the older of the two establishments and dates from around the 1820s. Neither Washington Street or Jane Street appear on the earliest street plan of the town, dated 1793, and were probably laid out around 1810-15. St Johns church is the oldest building in the street and was consecrated in 1814. Washington Street is named after George Washington.

*T*he north-west corner of Washington Street and Jane Street, *c.* 1935 and 2005. This set of photographs look in more detail at the New Crown Hotel, which once existed to the extreme right of the earlier photograph on the previous page, and the Washington Central Hotel which replaced it. Margaret Thornthwaite was one of the earliest licensees of the New Crown in the mid-1840s, although its actual date of construction is not clear. The New Crown was much larger than Old Crown on the opposite corner of Jane Street and occupied much the same area as the present Washington Central Hotel. The latter was built in the early 1980s by local motor dealer Bill Dobie. A decade later the popular hotel was greatly extended and its high square clock tower added. Today, it is the largest hotel in the town with a nightclub and health club. Initially it also accommodated a car showroom, located along the Jane Street façade in the area now occupied by Caesar's leisure club.

*L*ooking north along Washington Street from its junction with Jane Street, *c.* 1915 and 2005. The earlier photograph again reveals that Pow Street once extended across the end of Washington Street to the foot of Wilson Street and Ramsey Brow. The junction with Edkin Street can just be seen to the extreme left of the page. Edkin Street ran parallel to Jane Street through to the upper section of John Street: both streets have now disappeared.

Midway along on the right is the Theatre Royal, which opened around 1866, started life as the Lyceum and was probably built by George John Smith. Capable of holding around 400 people, the little Victorian theatre was leased annually to a succession of different managers. In 1912, Enrico Caruso performed there as part of the English Opera Company. The famous Italian tenor also visited the town's golf club and his name appears in their visitor's book.

Since 1936, the Theatre Royal has been the home of the Workington Playgoers Club.

*T*he Artillery Drill Hall in Edkin Street (now Risman Place) in 1915 and 2006. Completed in 1901, the Drill Hall on the north side of Edkin Street, extended along the rear boundary of St Johns Schools to the back of the former Workington Savings Bank in Pow Street. During the mid-1930s, after the bank moved to new premises in Murray Road, it was acquired as office accommodation for the Drill Hall. During the Second World War the 5th Battalion of the Border Regiment had its headquarters here. The substantial building with its iron-trussed roof was occasionally used for public dances and meetings. In 1967 the Borough Council acquired the premises and it was ultimately demolished to make way for the first town-centre redevelopment. The later photograph shows the new town centre as it approaches completion; in the distance we can just see Washington Street. This area is now known as Risman Place, named after another former Workington Town rugby league player, Gus Risman (1911-1994). As player coach he led Town to the famous victory in the 1952 Challenge Cup Final against Featherstone at Wembley.

*T*he mid-section of Jane Street, looking west towards Central Square, *c.* 1935 and 2005. The Oxford Cinema can be seen in the distance over the bridge and the large premises of the Workington and District Industrial and Provident Co-operative Society occupy both sides of the street at its junction with John Street. This busy street were once lined with shops, yet after the first redevelopment of the town centre in the early 1970s, the right side was demolished to make way for a large Co-op supermarket. This row of small shops was replaced by a long, virtually featureless, red-brick elevation, running almost the length of the street. Now isolated, the remaining shops in Jane Street suffered and the street lost much of its character.

Thirty years later, it is good to see that the latest development has resulted in the demolition of the supermarket and reinstatement of a more traditional looking streetscape.

*L*ooking south down Peter Street, *c.* 1960 and 2005. The bakery vans in the older photograph tell of a time when most large towns were served by a locally based co-operative society. The Workington and District Industrial and Provident Co-operative Society had its headquarters just around the corner in Jane Street, hence its name was often shortened to the 'Jane Street Co-op'. The Jane Street Co-op sold virtually everything from meat, fish and bread to coal. It had drapery, millinery, tailors and outfitters, furnishing and boot and shoe departments. Above the main shop was a large café, hall and a suite of rooms for weddings, dances and supper parties.

The single-storey building in the centre of these photographs is the former Co-op bakery, opened in 1933. A narrow lane runs down the side of the building to St Johns church and Washington Street.

*L*ooking north across Central Square, from the top of John Street, *c.* 1924 and 2005. The north side of this square was once dominated by the Central Hotel. It was established as a direct result of the opening of Workington's Central Railway Station on the west side of the square. Built originally in 1883, this hotel was acquired by Workington Brewery Co., who altered and extended it further in 1922. A prominent feature of the Central Hotel was its elaborate cast iron, glazed porch, which extended over the pavement and was supported by large and ornate cast iron columns. It was traditional for many years for people to gather in Central Square to see in the New Year. Large crowds would sing and dance, as church bells, works' hooters and ship's horns rang and sounded. The origins of these celebrations here may have begun with party-goers spilling into the street from the Central Hotel. Certainly, after the hotel was demolished in the late 1960s, the celebrations were never quite the same.

*L*ooking north across the junction of Oxford Street and Murray Road, *c.* 1955 and 2005. This part of the town is dominated by the imposing entrance to the bus station. Built in 1926 for Cumberland Motor Services Ltd, it was said to be the first covered bus station in England. Bus services were only introduced in the town after the end of the First World War, and by 1924 there was a regular timetable connecting Workington to other towns in West Cumbria and workers' buses transporting men from outlying areas, to and from the iron and steelworks. Today, bus services in our region are operated by Stagecoach, who acquired Cumberland Motor Services in the 1980s. Based in Perth, Stagecoach was started by the brother and sister partnership of Brian Souter and Ann Gloag and grew to massive proportions within just a few years. By the mid-1990s it operated in excess of 8,500 buses around the world. Adjacent to the bus station was Brownes Department store, built for the Whitehaven Beehive. Opened in November 1936, it sold a wide variety of goods from drapery and household furnishings to toys and kitchen utensils.

*L*ooking west along Murray Road, *c.* 1955 and 2005. This street in the centre of the town was only laid out in 1904, and takes its name from its owner and developer, William Murray. He also built the majority of the properties in Upton Street and Warwick Place. The projecting canopy of the Ritz cinema curving round into Upton Street is visible in the centre of the older photograph. Two large queues often formed outside the Ritz when a really popular film was screened. Braving the elements, one would stretch down this side of Murray Road, whilst the other extended along Upton Street and snaked round to the other side of the cinema.

On the right is one of the four lock-up shop units built at the same time as the cinema. This shop was a café and milk bar operated for many years by the Herbert family. One of the other shops in this row was Maycocks florists, run by the Green family. One of the oldest surviving businesses in town is John Walker's jewellers on the corner of Murray Road and Upton Street, directly opposite the entrance to the Ritz.

*T*he former post office, on the corner of Finkle Street and Murray Road, *c.* 1912 and 2005. This attractive red sandstone building dominates the junction of Pow Street and Finkle Street. Completed in 1904, it housed Workington's main post office for over ninety years. It also served as the town's sorting office until it was relocated to new premises in James Street, now occupied by G.H. Chambers & Sons. Today the sorting of the town's mail is carried out in a large industrial unit on Derwent Howe.

No. 21 Finkle Street, Workington, *c.* 1934 and 2005. Before there was national provision of power each town or district generally built its own gasworks and generated sufficient energy for its own consumers in the region. In Workington the supply of gas and electricity was the responsibility of the Borough Council. Gas was then traditionally produced by coal carbonisation, a method superseded by the widespread use of natural gas we know today. Prior to 1925, there was simply no electricity supply in the town and households had to rely on solid fuel or gas for all their heating, lighting and cooking. The town's first gasworks was established in Harrington Road in 1840 by a private company, but acquired by the Local Authority seven years later.

The older photograph shows the showroom opened in Finkle Street by the Borough Council in 1925 to display and market gas appliances. The gas supply remained under the control of the local authority until the gas industry was nationalised in 1949.

Memo from **J.T. Lister,** COMPLETE HOUSE FURNISHER. *Upholsterer Ironmonger, &c.*. Derwent Furnishing House, **WORKINGTON,**

*F*inkle Street, Workington, *c.* 1904 and 2005. Lister's original shop was located in these premises a little further along Finkle Street, almost opposite the old post office. Built around 1901, the property was constructed within the garden of Derwent House in Brow Top. Derwent House was built by the wealthy shipbuilder James Alexander (1799-1881) who occupied it until his death. When subsequently sold at auction the prospective buyers were made aware of the development potential of the rear garden frontage facing onto the now 'busy business thoroughfare' of Finkle Street. It was purchased by John Jessop, who had a house furnishers business on the corner of Sanderson Street and Washington Street. He was the father-in-law of John Thompson

Lister, who eventually took over the business following his death. After Listers moved to their present premises, at least part of their former shop was converted into a billiard hall. By the mid-1950s it had reverted to a furniture store operated by Simmons Ltd. Much of the original façade of this property still remains, although the ornate parapet wall and stonework at roof level has now been removed.

*L*ooking west along Finkle Street towards the former Wesleyan Methodist church (Trinity Methodist), *c.* 1910 and 2006. Of all the shopping streets in town this north side of Finkle Street has changed least since Victorian times. Originally, the main thoroughfare down to the harbour was along Brow Top, Derwent Street to Church Street, formally known as Priestgate. Finkle Street was then known as Back of Town and the gardens of the large houses on Brow Top extended onto what was once a narrow, unmade lane, with just a few cottages. By the 1870s, as the town expanded, the owners of the Brow Top properties sold off plots along the street, upon which were built shops. One exception was the plot behind

the arched opening in the centre of the older photograph. Work only began here during the summer of 2006 to develop this infill site. The Borough Council played an active role in widening Finkle Street in the 1890s, purchasing run-down cottages on the opposite side of the street and re-aligning this south side. The Carnegie Library and Theatre and the Appletree Hotel were later built here.

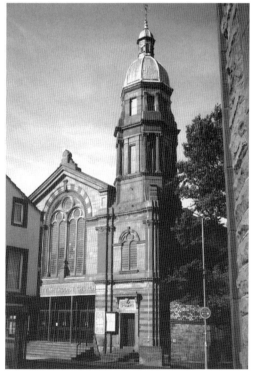

*T*he former Wesleyan Methodist church viewed from across South William Street, looking north from Vulcans Lane, *c.* 1892 and 2005. Although Wesleyan Methodism dates from May 1738, the date of establishment of the first congregation in town is not clear. Records suggest it was formed around 1767. We know John Wesley was a frequent visitor to West Cumberland and is thought to have visited Workington on at least two occasions. His first sermon was at the Assembly Rooms in Portland Square on 16 April 1761. The town's first chapel, located in Tiffen Lane at the rear of former Opera House, opened in 1792. They moved to an elegant new Georgian church, built here at the junction of South William Street and Finkle Street, in 1840. It was destroyed by fire in April 1889 and the present building, designed by Charles W. Bell, replaced it. The later photograph shows the glazed entrance doors and unsympathetic green slate panels on the lower section of the front elevation which were added during the mid-1960s.

*L*ooking almost due east from the end of South William Street, along Finkle Street, *c.* 1910 and 2005. Again we see the familiar landmark of Trinity Methodist church to the left of both photographs. On the opposite side of the South William Street is the former Congregational church (now United Reform). This attractive church was built in 1884, and replaced an older structure erected before 1786. At this time it was known as the Independent chapel or Low Meeting House. Workington's other independent chapel was the High Meeting house on the site of the former Presbyterian Church in Sanderson Street, which was demolished in recent years to make way for the Debenhams store. At the rear of the United Reform church is a small graveyard which faces onto Vulcans Lane.

Today it contains around twenty stones telling us that burials took place here from at least 1789 to 1966. A closer look at the earlier photograph reveals the location of the first W.H. Smith shop in town. Smith's initially operated a bookstall on the platform of the Low Railway Station. Later they moved to premises on the corner of John Street and Pow Street.

*R*ecent years have seen major improvements to Workington town centre, but secondary shopping areas such as Hagg Hill and Fisher Street have sadly slipped into decline. Prior to the 1860s, Hagg Hill (also known as Falcon Place) was simply an open space used primarily as a stone depot, with just a single dwelling near to the recently completed St Michael's School. Within a few years it grew rapidly into a prosperous and vibrant part of Victorian Workington with three large public halls. The Albert Hall on Fisher Street (now occupied by Macbeth & Son) was built in 1883 and could accommodate 600 people. After it was altered in 1935, it became a dance hall and billiard saloon. A little further down Fisher Street was Dent Hall (now the Gunners Club). One of its earlier proprietors was Christopher E. Edmundson who also ran one of the earliest dental practices in the town. Another public hall adjoined Whitfield's Arcade and became the Hippodrome cinema. All three halls were also used as venues for auction sales.

The view east along South William Street, from its junction with William Street, *c.* 1950 and 2005. South William Street runs from the Trinity Methodist church down to Fisher Street, which enters the north-east corner of Hagg Hill beside Dent Hall. The property with the bay windows on the right side of the photograph is Croft House, home of physician and surgeon Dr Charles McKerrow (1855-1940), who played a major role in establishing Workington Infirmary. He moved to the town in 1880 and for a short time was in partnership with Dr Alexander Hogg. In 1884, along with other doctors in the town, he joined a committee to build the town's first hospital. During the Victorian era the population had risen dramatically and the nearest hospitals were in Carlisle and Whitehaven. Workington Infirmary was opened in 1886 and Dr McKerrow was appointed first medical officer. In 1927, in partnership with his son Mungo and daughter Elizabeth (both qualified doctors), he opened the surgery in James Street.

*T*he north side of Fisher Street, viewed from the corner of South Watt Street, *c.* 1923 and 2005. The older photograph shows a bustling street contrasting with the later view of today looking quite neglected and almost insignificant. The demise was brought about by the redevelopment of the town centre during the late 1960s and the more recent increase in out-of-town retail outlets. Sadly, the majority of the shops in this part of Workington find day-to-day survival a real struggle. The end of Duke Street can be seen to the centre right of the both photographs. Here was Fox's grocers shop (now Macbeth & Son) in the premises adjoining the Albert Hall. Remarkably, on the corner of North Watt Street was also Walter Willsons and the Pent Stores, three more grocer's shops within a few yards of each other. Shopping patterns have changed so much in the last few decades.

*F*lacon Place (also known as Hagg Hill),
c. 1904. Just fifty years or so before this
photograph was taken, Hagg Hill was simply
an open space, crossed by a narrow, unmade
track leading to the church, following much
the same line as today's Fisher Street. By the
mid-1880s, it had become a busy shopping
area for the hundreds of newly built terraced

houses in adjoining streets. From 1883
twice-weekly markets were held here which
continued until the 1980s.

Whitfield's Arcade, to the right of the
picture, was opened by James Whitfield
in 1886 and was home to a number of
permanent shops or stallholders. Its entrance
below the clock faced onto the gable end of

St Michaels School. The
arcade extended along
Station Road, through
to and along the west
side of South Watt
Street. The building also
contained a large public
hall often used as an
auction room and was
eventually converted into
the Hippodrome cinema,
with a dance hall in the
basement.

*S*t Michaels parish church and graveyard, viewed from Hagg Hill, *c.* 1904 and 2005. A place of worship may have existed here since at least the eighth century. Stone sculptures found here tell us a great deal about the earliest inhabitants of the town. Anglo-Saxon detailing has been found and others confirm the existence of a later Norse or Viking community. The major difference between these photographs is the absence of stones and memorials within its graveyard.

In 1954, the burial ground at St Michaels was conveyed to the Borough Council, who took over responsibility for its maintenance. They subsequently removed the majority of the stones to make grass cutting simpler; from around eight hundred memorials, recording the family history of many generations of townspeople, fewer than eighty remain.

*L*ooking west down Station Road towards Workington Low Railway Station, *c.* 1910 and 2005. The junction with Dean Street can be seen to the right of the photographs. Early maps of the town tell us this road was originally called Cooke Lane and only ran from Hagg Hill down to Falcon Street. The present street name was adopted in 1883 when it was decided to extend the road all the way up to Jane Street. It received its new name by virtue of there being a railway station at each end of the street. Workington Low Station, the town's first (and now only remaining) railway station opened during the late 1840s, whilst Workington Central Station in Central Square had been open just a couple of years.

As the road was nearing completion, the Borough Council changed their minds and decided to call the central section of the new road Oxford Street. The later picture reveals this once prominent shopping street is now almost devoid of any shops. The majority of its neat Victorian shop fronts have been removed and the properties converted to other uses.

*T*he south side of Station Road, viewed from the junction with Hagg Hill, *c.* 1903 and 2005. This block of property running from the corner of Senhouse Street to the corner of Lonsdale Street is now a shadow of its former self. It lies dilapidated and its demolition is imminent. At one time it was an elegant row of shops. Of particular interest is the shop to the far left of the photographs: this was occupied for many years by Joseph Goss' grocers. It was the first of four such shops in the town operated by this family firm. Their other shops were in Pow Street, Harrington Road and Moss Bay Road. When this Station Road shop eventually closed in the 1970s, some of its old shop fittings are believed to have been acquired by the Beamish Museum in the north east.

*T*he former Town Hall in Oxford Street, *c.* 1934 and 2005. This property was formerly an elegant house called Shrub Hill encircled by open fields and standing in relative isolation, well away from the hustle and bustle of the town. The only development looking south was the abandoned pitheads and spoil heaps of Elizabeth and Hope pits, located on the other side of where Vulcans park now stands. To reach the house one travelled down a long drive called Lowsa Lane which began almost at the junction of Fisher Street and South William Street, following the line of what is now Park Lane. At its entrance was a small single-storey gatehouse, which still survives today at the rear of the Waverley Hotel.

The property was later renamed Field House, after it was aquired by the local engineering contractor Richard Harrison Hodgson. In 1899, it was sold to the Workington Borough Council and subsequently converted for use as a town hall. Today it is owned by Allerdale Borough Council and used as office accomodation.

3

Beyond the Heart of the Town

*T*he two tall stone chimneys and the castellated oval engine house at Jane Pit are virtually all that remains of Workington's once rich coal industry, an industry that was until the latter part of the nineteenth century of primary commercial importance and without which iron and steel production, our harbour and town itself may never really have developed. Jane Pit was sunk in 1843 by the Curwen family, who then owned all the town's mineral rights to the south of the River Derwent. For centuries, earlier generations of the family had made a fortune by expoiting these abundant coal reserves. The town's last working pit was Solway colliery, situated a stone's throw from Jane Pit to the south-west of the Ellis Sports Ground. It was operated by United Steel Companies, who also owned the iron and steel plant on the opposite side of the main Whitehaven to Workington railway line. Work to sink this pit began in 1937 although it did not come into full production until the end of the Second World War. Much of the coal extracted here was transported over the railway line on an overhead conveyor to be converted into coke. This was used to smelt iron in the companies' blast furnaces. In 1947, ownership of the Solway colliery passed to the National Coal Board when the industry was nationalised. Production continued until 1973 before the pit was finally closed.

*L*ooking down High Street from the corner of Ashfield Road, *c.* 1913 and 2005. This area of Workington was once commonly known as Uppergate or Townhead, but both names disappeared from use well before the 1950s. These substantial three-storey houses (or villas as they were then called) with their finely detailed and well proportioned stonework façades are regarded as some of the most attractive Victorian homes in the town. Here were the residences of some of the more wealthy and prominent townspeople, such as Joseph Huntrods (1852-1923). He was managing director of Kirk Brothers Iron foundries and ran a substantial ship chandlers and mill furnishers business on the corner

of Station Road and Falcon Street. He was also chairman of the Workington Bridge and Boiler Company and a director of the Whitehaven Iron & Steel Co. Huntrods was a successful and much travelled man, making several trips to the United States and Canada. He is also believed to have invested in Peter Kirk's attempts to build a new steel plant near Seattle, based on Workington's Moss Bay works.

*T*he front elevation of Elm Bank in High Street, *c.* 1892 and 2006. This property is one of the oldest remaining in this part of the town. One of its earliest occupiers, when the house was much smaller, was John Allan, a blacksmith, cartwright and gig maker. It was probably extended by the wealthy ship owner Henry Grayson who lived here with his large family from the 1850s. During the 1870s it was the home of Joseph Ledger, chairman of the Moss Bay Haematite Iron & Steel Co. He ranks alongside the likes of Messrs Valentine, Kirk, Ellis and Duffield, all of whom played a prominent role in iron and steel manufacture in Workington. From the 1880s, banker and magistrate Robert Steele Thompson occupied the house. He was manager of the Cumberland Union Bank until 1875 and the old photograph probably shows the Thompson family playing croquet on the lawn.

*B*ankfield Mansion, looking from the south east, *c.* 1913 and 2005. With the exception of Workington Hall, Bankfield was once the most prominent house in the town. This elegant property was in fact two large, semi-detached houses with separate entrances at each end. Visitors to both houses entered the estate through the gates at the south end of Bank Road and to reach the house, they climbed a steep drive through the wooded grounds. The tradesman's entrance was off Newlands Lane, down a cobbled lane which is still visible today. Bankfield was built in 1876 by local contractor Richard W. Schofield, for local ironmasters, Peter Kirk and Charles Valentine. Both houses later passed to the Iredale family, who operated Workington Brewery. During the First World War the property became an auxiliary hospital and cared for around 260 wounded servicemen. It was subsequently acquired by Workington Borough Council, who leased it to the National Coal Board. After their departure the once grand house fell into disrepair and Bankfield was demolished in 1980.

*M*oss Bay Iron and Steelworks, viewed from the south east, *c.* 1895 and 2005. During the latter half of the nineteenth century, Workington became a major centre for the production of iron and steel. It was an industry that grew rapidly to employ thousands of people and was primarily responsible for the development and growth of the town and its port.

Prior to the formation of the Workington Iron & Steel Co. in 1909, iron and steel was manufactured on several sites across the town, each run as an independent concern. The Moss Bay Iron and Steel Co. started life as the Moss Bay Haematite Ironworks in 1872. It was established by Peter Kirk and Charles Valentine, who operated the smaller Quayside Forge in Stanley Street. Steelmaking began here in June 1877 and the first rail was produced two months later. Ironmaking ceased in the town over twenty-five years ago and steel-rail production came to an end in August 2006. Corus Rail then transferred its operation to a new plant at their Scunthorpe works, marking the final demise of an industry that had shaped so much of the town's past.

The site of the former Derwent Ironworks, *c.* 1979 and 2005. The earlier photograph records the last few days of the Derwent blast furnaces as their demolition progressed. Pig-iron production began here in 1875 and was smelted on this site for another century. Originally these works, just a few hundred yards north of the Moss Bay plant,

were operated by the Derwent Haematite Iron Co. and later purchased by Wilson Cammell & Co, (of Dronfield, near Sheffield) who moved their entire operation here in 1883. Upwards of two thousand people left the once thriving Derbyshire town and moved north to settle in Workington. The 'Dronnies', as they became known, were initially greeted with some hostility by the local people. They were considered more skilled and were often better paid, and their arrival *en masse* resulted in higher rents and rising prices. It took some time for the two communities to become fully integrated. Like the Moss Bay works, Cammell's was eventually amalgamated into the Workington Iron & Steel Co in 1909.

*T*he rail finishing plant at Moss Bay, viewed from the east, *c.* 1960 and 2005. In the foreground is the main Harrington-Workington railway line. In 1919, a decade after its creation, the Workington Iron & Steel Co. was taken over by the rapidly expanding Sheffield-based United Steel Group, later United Steel Companies. By the end of the Second World War, with the assistance of substantial government investment, Workington possessed one of the most advanced steel-making plants in Europe, if not the world. The town's iron and steel works remained in the hands of United Steel until the industry was nationalised in July 1967. The plant was thereafter operated by the newly-created British Steel Corporation. Workington is still, at least for the time being, a centre for steel rail production and throughout its long history has supplied many thousands of miles of track to almost every rail network in the world. As the Moss Bay plant closes, the townspeople are justifiably proud of its rich industrial past.

The old Workington Infirmary, 1895 and 2005. The early photograph, taken from Harrington Road cemetery, records the laying of the foundation stone in August 1885. The ceremony was performed by Edward Darcy Curwen and construction work took almost fifteen months. This was the town's first hospital and was funded by donations from the more affluent townspeople and the local iron and steel plants, who were the driving force behind its construction. Over half a century before the NHS, it was also primarily supported by voluntary contributions from the workers in the district.

Although the infirmary was extended many times, the later photograph records the oldest, 1885 section of the building, which housed the original three wards and contained twelve male and four female beds. Then the staff consisted of just one matron, assisted by a single day and night nurse. When the town's health care was transferred to the new community hospital in Park Lane the property was demolished.

*T*he old Workington Infirmary and the new Community Hospital, 2005. The larger photograph shows the Outpatients department of the recently demolished Workington Infirmary, viewed from the foot of Honister Drive. The other photograph shows the new Community Hospital in Park Lane, built to replace the infirmary, upon the site of the town's Technical College. The site of the old hospital, which when it closed extended from the rear of Harrington Road Cemetery and Frostoms Road, across the old Cleator and Workington railway line and up to Mason Street, is to become a housing development. The foundation stone for the new Community Hospital was officially laid by Dale Campbell Savors in January 2004.

The building was officially opened by Tony Cunningham on 1 April 2005.

Workington's fire brigade, *c.* 1914 and 2005. The earlier photograph shows the town's Merryweather Motor Fire Engine, acquired in 1913, outside the old fire station in Harrington Road. This was opposite the present St Joseph's School, on the site of the Charters Close housing development. This relatively new fire engine with its highly polished brass-finished radiator shell and headlamps replaced the brigade's antiquated horse-drawn pump, which had been in service for almost twenty years. The brigade was then operated by the Borough Council and manned by volunteers recruited from their staff and the local police force. Workington's fire service was absorbed into the newly created Cumberland fire service during the early years of the Second World War and moved to the present fire station at the top of King Street. Today, it employs a staff of full-time fire-fighters and has three fire engines at its disposal.

*L*ooking south-east across Millfield to Workington Hall Mill, *c.* 1910 and 2006. The substantial building to the left of both photographs is a former manorial watermill. It is believed to have existed on this site since at least the mid-thirteenth century and was probably built by Patric de Curwen, who granted the monks of St Bees Abbey the privilege of receiving '14 salmon yearly to be obtained from the pool' of his Workington mill, 'by the hand of his miller'. It was driven by at least two undershot timber waterwheels, one wheel fixed externally and another contained within the mill and both fed from the millrace. This still winds its way from the Yearl, across Hall Park and the Cloffolks before draining into the South Gut, below St Michael's church. Today, the waterwheels are no longer in place and the building has been converted into a dwelling. You can still see marks inscribed by the old wheel on the outside of the thick stone walls.

The front elevation of Workington Hall, viewed from the south, *c.* 1892 and 2005. Workington Hall was the ancestral home of the influential Curwen family, lords of the manor of Workington for almost eight hundred years. It was built by Sir Gilbert Curwen, the great grandson of Patric Curwen, who erected the first house on the site, some half a century earlier. Previously the family had resided at Burrow on the opposite side of the River Derwent. At this time King John was on the English throne and the English-Scottish border lands had lapsed into a further state of unrest. Cumberland was subjected to frequent Border Reviver raids and attacks. There is little doubt that the elevated site of the hall was chosen as it was defensively stronger and commanded unrestricted views up the Derwent valley and over the estuary towards the Solway Firth.

Workington Hall, viewed from the west, c. 1892 and 2005. To the far right of the earlier photograph, we can see part of the original thirteenth-century pele tower. The front, ivy clad sections of the hall date from the end of the eighteenth century. This work was initially started by Henry Curwen and completed after his death by his son-in-law, John Christian Curwen. Eminent architect John Carr (of York) was responsible for remodelling the hall, transforming it into a stylish Georgian mansion house. Much of his work, particularly his interiors, was influenced by his famous contemporary Robert Adam with whom he had worked. After the Second World War Workington Hall was allowed to fall into disrepair and became the roofless ruin we see today. Many significant features were lost, including all Carr's finely detailed interiors.

*C*uckoo Arch, on the Stainburn Road, *c.* 1892 and 2005. Although it disappeared around seventy years ago, the bridge framed by the adjoining woodland has featured on countless old picture postcards and been photographed or painted by numerous local people. This semi-circular stone-built arch once spanned the road from Workington to Stainburn, just to the east of the entrance to Stainburn School. It was built around 1795 by John Christian Curwen from the stone quarried at Schoose, and provided a direct link from the grounds of Workington Hall to his Schoose Farm estates on the opposite side of the road and then up Gildergill and through the golf course to another of the family farms at Hunday. The arch was demolished in 1931, its condition having deteriorated and its narrow opening creating a hazard to traffic using this once busy road.

*L*ooking west along the South Quay at Harrington Harbour, 1902 and 2005. Things have come almost full circle: when Henry Curwen built the first wharf here in 1770 there was not a single house in this area, yet by the end of the eighteenth century a community of narrow streets had sprung up around the port, rows of terraced houses built almost on the harbour side where a thousand

people lived and worked within yards of the busy quayside. It is almost impossible to believe now so many dwellings once existed in this area, as only one remains. This was once the former Ship Inn, which is now a private house and stands in isolation on the South Quay. The harbour was created to export coal from Harrington Colliery, transported

to waiting ships over an inclined wagon way which followed the line of William Street.. The rails of this wagon way are seen emerging onto the quayside to the left of the earlier picture.

A view looking east from the West Quay across the empty Inner Harbour at Harrington, c. 1930 and 2005. The earlier photograph was probably taken shortly after the port of Harrington was closed in 1928. The last commercial vessel to sail from the harbour was the *Girasol*, a steam coaster loaded with 250 tons of pitch for Swansea. The once bustling quaysides now lie quiet and deserted. To the right of the picture we see some of the properties that once existed at the east end of Quay Street, which ran almost the full length of the South Quay.

This is the oldest part of the harbour and where Henry Curwen (of Workington Hall) built his first wharf in 1770. Annually from here, thousands of tons of coal were once loaded into hundreds of waiting ships. In these early years, Harrington Harbour was widely known as 'Bellaport'. This name was probably chosen by Henry Curwen in honour of his wife Isabella, although some believe it may well have been named after his only surviving daughter, also called Isabella. Of all the West Cumbrian ports, this once thriving and important harbour is now a mere shadow of its former self.

4

The Harbour and along the River Derwent

The town's harbour at the mouth of the River Derwent has a long and varied history going back over five centuries. John Leland, the King's Antiquary, visited the town around 1535 and referred to it as a 'pretty fysher town'. Herring fishing was then the principle activity although the town had little more than a handful of boats. Besides fresh, salted and pickled herring, these catches were also smoked before being taken south to ports such as Chester and Liverpool. There was no wharf or quayside and vessels would moor alongside the south bank of the river to discharge their cargoes. With the increase in coal production, much of which was exported to Ireland, the harbour around the South Gut was improved and developed. Iron and steel brought greater prosperity to the port and Lonsdale Dock was built on the north side of the estuary during the 1860s. This was replaced by the Prince of Wales Dock, opened in 1927. Today in order to survive the port has diversified into handling other goods. There is now very little fishing, no coal exports and the last ship to carry steel rails from the port departed in October 2006.

*L*ooking east along the South Gut of Workington harbour, 1837 and 2005. The South quay to the right of both pictures is the oldest part of the harbour, the first wharf being built here around the end of the seventeenth century. Prior to this, goods were simply transferred on and off vessels from the river bank. This is confirmed on the earliest map of the town, dated 1569. The tower of St Michaels church has stood since the turbulent times of the Border feuds. Perhaps the church bell was rung to signal an alarm to the townspeople when Scottish invaders were sighted in the Solway. Despite two disastrous fires at the parish church this square fortress-like tower still survives. The earlier illustration also shows the Georgian-style church which was destroyed by fire in 1887.

*L*ooking east along the south quay of the Lonsdale (now the Prince of Wales) Dock, *c.* 1890 and 2006. The Lonsdale Dock on the north side of the River Derwent was constructed by William, Lord Lonsdale, after whom it was named. Completed in 1862 it was Workington's first deep-water dock and was intended to cater for the rapidly expanding iron and steel plants built on Oldside. It was soon realised that it was too small and its entrance on the north bank of the river was so poorly designed that long steamers often found it impossible to negotiate. The dock gates of the old Lonsdale Dock can be seen almost in the centre of the earlier photograph, whilst to the left is a sailing ship moored inside the dock. The river channel is to the right just out of view.

When the Prince of Wales Dock was built, much of the original Lonsdale Dock structure was retained at its east end.

A view looking east towards the entrance to the South Gut, *c.* 1915 and 2005. Prior to the construction of the Prince of Wales Dock, the entrance to the South Gut was open and unrestricted. Today it is spanned by a railway bridge which was erected to provide the dock with a more direct link to the iron and steel plants south of the River Derwent.

Much of the town's production was now centred here and previously all rail traffic to the dock had to use the main Whitehaven to Maryport line and cross the river to Oldside, before being shunted south to the harbour.

Unlike today, the tall cargo schooners such as the one shown in the earlier photograph could continue to use the South Gut, as the entire bridge structure originally swung through 90 degrees to allow these larger vessels in and out of the tidal dock. In 1981, this swing bridge was replaced with the modern fixed railway bridge.

The Workington Lifeboat, c. 1890 and 2006. The town's first lifeboat station was opened in 1886 by the Royal National Lifeboat Institution following the wreck of the schooner *Margaret* (of Ramsey), which was lost with all hands. Previously, any vessel in trouble had to rely upon either the town's Rocket Brigade or other lifeboats stationed at Maryport or Whitehaven. The earlier photograph probably depicts *Dodo*, the town's first lifeboat, which was provided from a legacy of the Harrison family. This relatively small vessel had no engine, her only form of propulsion being oar and sail. The self-righting wooden boat, with a crew of around a dozen men, remained in service until 1899 when she was replaced by a similar vessel of the same name. By comparison today's lifeboat, the Sir John Fisher (47-028) is a steel-hulled 14.3 metres (46.91ft) long all-weather vessel, which is usually manned by a crew of six or seven. Capable of a top speed of seventeen knots, the Tyne-class lifeboat has a range of 240 nautical miles. It is usually launched from the lifeboat station gantry crane on the north side of the Prince of Wales dock gates.

*L*ooking seaward to the Solway, along the southern side of the Prince of Wales Dock, *c.* 1926 and 2005. The Prince of Wales Dock on the north side of the River Derwent estuary was build to the west of the smaller Lonsdale Dock, which had been constructed in 1861. It was formally opened by the Prince of Wales (later King Edward VIII) on 30 June 1927, after whom it was named. The construction of the town's new wet dock was funded by the Workington Iron & Steel Co., a branch of United Steel Companies. The completion of the Prince of Wales Dock, with its far superior facilities, spelt the decline and ultimate demise of neighbouring ports such as Maryport and Harrington. Until recent

years its primary exports have always been steel rails and sleepers, billets and bars, pig iron and coal, while prior to the closure of the town's blast furnaces in the 1980s, iron ore was imported in huge quantities. With the dramatic decline of the town's heavy industries, the port has diversified into handling other cargoes. They have also established a container-handling facility on the north quay.

*L*ooking south-east across the Prince of Wales Dock, *c.*1950 and 2006. The earlier photograph shows a busy bustling scene, with at least six or seven boats moored along the quaysides, quite a contrast to the later picture. The row of steam coasters to the left are moored in the widest corner of the dock and are probably awaiting cargoes of coal. The coaster with the white band around its funnel and painted with the letter M was operated by Munroe Bros. This Liverpool based company worked the Irish coal trade and the North Wales slate trade. The two larger vessels on the opposite quayside are located in an area which was once the Lonsdale Dock and were probably discharging iron ore. Today, barely 250 vessels visit the Prince of Wales annually, albeit they are much larger ships. Two of the principle cargoes now handled are Gypsum and Perlite imported from Spain. These are transported inland to British Gypsum's works at Kirkby Thore. Perlite is being unloaded in the recent photograph from *John-Paul K*, registered in Delfzijl.

*J*ohn Pier on the south side of the estuary, *c.* 1925 and 2006. This breakwater was built between 1824-25 in an attempt to protect the river estuary from silting up. It cost around £7,000 and was funded by John Christain Curwen and public subscriptions. Forty years later John Pier had become ineffective as the shoreline had built up either side of the breakwater and the harbour channel was again under threat. Thousands of tons of slag waste tipped on the foreshore by the steelwarts compounded the problem. Initially it was proposed to extend the structure but eventually it was decided to build the present concrete breakwater further north. John Pier with its substantial square stone platform eventually became isolated from the sea as the new breakwater pushed the shoreline further west. It was finally demolished when the coastline was landscaped after the closure of the steelworks. The later photograph shows the seaward end of the present breakwater which marks the end of the C2C cycle route.

*L*ooking west along the south side of the River Derwent towards John Pier, *c.* 1900 and 2005. To many this set of photographs shows what they believe to be 'Billy Bumley' house. But this structure has inherited the name of an earlier beehive-like landmark which stood high upon the shore hills and was once used by mariners to plot their course to and from the port. It was demolished in the 1960s by the Workington Iron & Steel Co. who owned the site and claimed the building had become unsafe. Its actual location is now difficult to determine following extensive landscaping after the closure of the ironworks in the 1970s. The existing circular building originally served as a shelter for the tide watcher who was responsible for hoisting

and lowering the large red ball up and down the tall flagpole-like structure, seen in the centre of the older photograph, to indicate the depth of water in the harbour entrance.

Workington Tug-Boat. S.S. Weathercock.

The Workington Tug Boat, *c.* 1925 and 2006. The earlier photograph shows the SS *Weathercock* approaching the Lonsdale Dock with the chimneys of the Oldside and Lonsdale Ironworks visible in the distance. The majority of larger vessels using the port need assistance in and out of the harbour. Over the years the town has had a tug on permanent duty. One of the earliest was a paddle-driven steam tug which was generally moored alongside the South Quay. Early photographs record graceful sailing ships being hauled along the river channel by this tug. The later photograph shows the present class IX tug the *Derwent*, built by Dutch Damen and acquired by the port in 1993. This powerful multi-purpose vessel operates as both a tug and a pilot boat and can also be adapted as a plough dredger. Today, towage is normally required for vessels over 92 metres or as directed by the Harbour Master. Vessels over 50 metres are also required to use the pilot to guide and direct them into and out of the harbour.

V iew looking south west across the Cloffolks, with Brow Top in the distance, *c.* 1850 and 2006. The early picture is from an engraving published by Workington bookseller John Mordy. It is particularly interesting as it depicts the Cloffolks as a green open space before the railway embankment was built in the late 1870s. The large properties on Brow Top were once the residences of prominent townspeople. Derwent House, almost on the corner of Speedwell Lane, can be seen to the left of the earlier photograph. Built in the early 1840s this house was the home of shipbuilder James Alexander (1799-1881). He ran a shipyard on the south side of the estuary, near the Dock Quay. He is credited with building many graceful timber sailing ships, including the *Christabel*, a 335-ton barque, the first vessel of Liverpool's famous Lamport & Holt line. He also built the *Workington,* a 150-ton brig launched on 2 Nov 1840. Derwent House can just be seen in the later photograph rising above the trees. It is now forms the rear section of the Poundstretcher store in Finkle Street.

*T*he view east across the Cloffolks in 1903 and 2005. The Cloffolks was once a very much larger, flatter area than we know today. Before the three sports stadia of Lonsdale, Borough and Derwent Parks and the cricket field were laid out, this space extended from the eastern end of the South Gut almost to Hall Park and from the south

bank of the River Derwent to the steep incline below Brow Top. There were once streets and houses here, built on either side of Dolly Brow (the lower end of William Street). They occupied much of the area between Derwent Street and Church Street over to the small stream or beck running across the Cloffolks, the course of which has been changed in the last half century or so.

We can see some of these properties to the right of the earlier photograph, which was taken during that year's Uppies and Downies contest. From the beginning of the last century much of the Cloffolks was utilised as the town's refuse tip and this landfill has artificially raised several areas.

*A*nother view of Cloffolks, this time looking south towards Derwent Street, 1903 and 2005. The earlier photograph, again taken during the Uppies and Downies contest, shows more of the properties that once existed on the Cloffolks. Streets such as Griffin Street, Hayton Square, Skinners Lane and Bells Lane are now just a fading memory. There were also a number of smaller houses built on the steep sloping bank from Derwent Street down to Griffin Street. These included a mass of little cottages known as the Brows, with had few basic facilities and were closely huddled together with only the odd house having a back yard. The Brows were reached from very narrow steep, cobbled lanes and long flights of stone steps. These unfit properties, once home to nearly eighty families, were demolished in the 1920s, the inhabitants being rehoused by the Corporation.

*L*ooking west towards the High Brewery from below Hall Brow, *c.* 1953 and 2005. When this brewery was established towards the end of the eighteenth century, the town already had two other brewers. The oldest was the Low Brewery, which was located in Griffin Street on the Cloffolks, whilst the other belonged to the Curwen family and stood in the grounds of Workington Hall, close to the entrance to Hall Park and almost opposite the former Forge Hammer public house. The High Brewery, under the control of several generations of the Iredale family, eventually became known as the Workington Brewery Co. and continued to operate until the 1980s. Many of the town's older residents still recall the sweet smell of the brewery drifting through the town streets. The company was famous for its John Peel brand ales which were available throughout West Cumbria and beyond. The company was acquired by the Lancashire brewers Matthew Brown Ltd, who were themselves later taken over by Scottish & Newcastle. This spelled the end of brewing in the town and the building with its familiar square, eight-storey tower which dominates the town's landscape lay vacant for many years.

Another view of the square tower of Workington Brewery, looking from Ladies Walk, 1997 and 2005. The earlier photograph shows the old brewery in a poor state of repair. Today, just over a century after the tower of this historic building was built, it has been extensively restored and has a new use. A sympathetic renovation funded by Impact housing has transformed the brewery into an attractive housing scheme. The development, which has retained many features of the original Victorian brewery such as exposed beams and cast-iron columns, has created a number of unusual and quite unique apartments. At the top of the distinctive old tower is a penthouse with the master bedroom at its highest point surrounded on all four sides by windows. Those living in the upper levels also enjoy outstanding views across the River Derwent valley.

*L*ooking south west towards Workington Bridge, 1892 and 2005. This substantial stone road bridge was completed in 1841 and replaced an earlier structure located a few hundreds yards upstream. Records suggest that there has been a bridge over the Derwent here since at least the twelfth century. To the right of the earlier photograph is the signal box of Workington Bridge Station built against the parapet wall of the bridge. From here you could board trains to Cockermouth and beyond and travel on the Cockermouth & Workington railway, opened in 1847. The tracks eastward ran alongside the north side of the river until they reached Barepot.

This railway station was one of three that served the town; only the Low Station now survives. Today, some forty years after the line closed, nature has reclaimed the site of the old station and it is impossible to photograph the scene from the same location. However, the later photograph, taken closer to the riverbank, shows in detail the three finely dressed stonework arches.

5

Railways – All Change

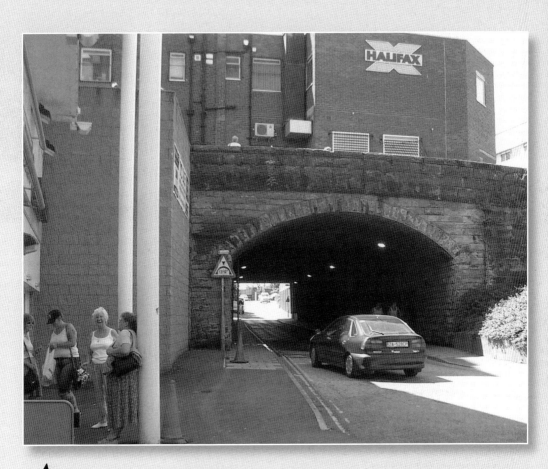

A closer look beneath Pow Street reveals the stonework arch of an old bridge that is a further reminder that a railway once ran through the centre of the town. Many vehicles now pass back and forth through this underpass each and every day to get to the Cloffolks car park, but few drivers will remember that the tracks of the Cleator & Workington Junction Railway once followed the same course. The bridge, built in 1878, has gradually become a tunnel as more and more properties have been built over the railway cutting around Pow Street, Finkle Street and Murray Road junction. The photographs on page 10 and 12 describe the scene at street level in more detail.

*F*ront elevation of Workington's Low Railway Station, *c.* 1910 and 2006. This attractive yellow brickwork building, with its fine detailing, was built in 1886. It replaced a very basic single-storey structure which had stood for nearly forty years. This was located further north of the present station opposite where Belle Isle Place once stood. To the right of both photographs are the approaches of the road bridge crossing over the line to the harbour and Derwent How, curving round to Church Street. This substantial bridge is often referred to locally as 'the Viaduct'. It was built at the same time as the existing Victorian station and replaced a simple level crossing which allowed carts and pedestrians to cross directly from the foot of Station Road into Stanley Street.

*L*ooking north along the east platform of Workington Low Station, *c.* 1910 and 2005. The line from Whitehaven running through the town and north to Maryport was built by the Whitehaven Junction Railway. It opened in January 1846 and was the first railway into the town. Twenty years later it was acquired by the powerful London North Western Railway which had its headquarters at Euston Station. At the same time they also took control of the Cockermouth and Workington Railway, running east towards the Lake District. In the early photograph the LNWR station staff pose in front of the W.H. Smith & Sons news stand. The bookstall may have gone, but the glazed roof running the length of the platform is still supported by the single row of original Victorian cast-iron columns. A closer look at the signage along the platform reminds us that there were once separate waiting rooms for first and third class passengers and for gentlemen and ladies.

W orkington's Motive Power depot, adjacent to the Low Station, 2005 and 2006. Situated just a few hundred yards south of the station was another reminder of just how much the railways have changed since the dramatic cuts of the 1960s. Within this massive Victorian engine shed upwards of thirty steam locomotives were once repaired and maintained. The early photograph taken shortly before the shed was dismantled reveals that it was still remarkably intact, despite closing in 1968 and lying vacant for almost forty years. Several hundred men were once employed here in its heyday, and it was haunting to stand within the empty shell of the building and imagine the smells, the noise and the rows of steam locomotives. The later photograph shows the final stages of its

demolition. The structure will be preserved at the Grand Central Station at Loughborough where it is to be re-erected. The Leicestershire-based team spent a great deal of time measuring and photographing the building before work began to dismantle it.

A view of the exterior of the Workington Motive Power Depot looking north, *c.* 1962 and 2005. Continuing on from the previous page we take a further look at the building. The early photograph records the once so very common sight of rows of steam locomotives outside the engine shed. This is a sight railway enthusiasts would die for today, yet until its closure, the residents of the houses on both sides of the station witnessed the scene day in day out for decades. A variety of locomotives were once based here, used for hauling both freight and passenger trains. These included Ivatt class 2 and 4, Black 5 and Stanier. The massive engine shed was divided with a wall down the centre, with five roads (or tracks) either side. The most recent photograph shows the track bed overgrown and the building shortly before it was dismantled. The Loughborough project received around £100,000 from the Railway Heritage Trust to assist the work. Part of this funding will be used to capture the memories of those who worked within the Workington shed.

*L*ooking north towards Workington's Central Station, *c.* 1935 and 2006. The other railway through the town was the Cleator & Workington Junction Railway, opened in 1878. The line was predominately built to provide a more direct route between the rich iron ore mines in and around Cleator and the town's ironworks at Oldside and Moss Bay. Central Station to the right of the earlier photograph was the headquarters of the C&WJR and was located on the south side of Oxford Street just off Central Square. On the opposite platform was a single-storey, timber shelter and a square water tank. Steam locomotives halted here to take on water. The tracks can be seen curving gently from the left, through the station and under the bridge below Oxford Street. The later photograph reveals how little now remains of the old station with the exception of the bridge and its long parapet wall. The road through what is now the Central car park follows much the same line as the old tracks before descending down an incline beneath Pow Street en route north. The last passenger train to use the station ran in April 1931.

*T*he view south down Harrington Road from the bottom of Mason Street and John Street, *c.* 1919 and 2005. This bridge across Harrington Road was built in 1877-78 and carried the tracks of the Cleator & Workington Junction Railway to and from Central Station. The line from Cleator Moor descended through Distington, Harrington and Westfield and emerged at this point from a deep cutting beside the old infirmary. Unfortunately, with the increase in traffic along Harrington Road, the narrow and low-arched bridge became difficult to negotiate, particularly for double-decker buses. They could only safely pass through the centre of the bridge, restricting the carriageway for other users. One veteran bus driver tells how they were warned to 'line the radiator cap of their vehicle up with the white line down the centre of the road' to prevent a collision with the bridge. The bridge was eventually demolished in 1981 by the County Council and the road widened.

*R*ailway engines at Workington, *c.* 1962 and 2006. In four decades the locomotives serving the town have changed so much. The earlier photograph shows a 2-6-0 class 4F, ex-London Midland Scottish steam locomotive. Introduced in 1947, this powerful engine was once used to haul both passenger and freight trains. It is seen moving along the tracks to the west side of the old Motive Power Depot at Workington, now demolished. By the 1960s, steam locomotives were gradually phased out. The later picture shows a Northern Rail diesel passenger train passing the same spot, *en route* south to Barrow.

6

Lost Churches and Schools

*P*upils of Workington's St John School pose for a group photograph in their classroom, *c.* 1925. This school opened in 1860 and was located in the upper section of John Street. It was demolished during the late 1960s to make way for the building of St John's Shopping Precinct. Its pupils transferred to the new Ashfield Infants and Junior Schools, built at the end of Newlands Lane. The classroom in this photograph is so different from today's. All the scholars then sat side by side on long bench seats in galleries (or tiers) facing their teacher. Within a few years this system of seating, which had been common throughout the town's schools since Victorian times,

was replaced with rows of new desks. These dual desks, with heavy cast-iron frames, had a thick hardwood work surface and seat. Workington's Victorian schools were originally administered by a locally based School Board made up of local councillors, the clergy and prominent members of the community. In August 1903 this was replaced by the Borough of Workington Education Commitee, which later had its offices at Mossdale House on Harrington Road. Responsibility for the town's education finally passed to the Cumberland Education Authority and Workington became part of the western area, administered from the same office.

W orkington's Baptist church on Harrington Road, *c.* 1892 and 2006. Completed in 1886, this church replaced the Baptist mission room in Edkin Street. The new church was required as the influx of migrant steelworkers from Dronfield swelled the congregation to such a degree that the Edkin Street premises proved inadequate.

The building, with its twin pepper-pot towers, once dominated the corner of Gray Street and Harrington Road. It was demolished in the early 1980s and a smaller church was built on the open area of land to the right of the old photograph. To fund the new church a number of new flats and houses were built on the site of the old one. All that remains of the nineteenth-century building is a single, square sandstone gate post against the gable end of the older terraced houses, seen to the left of the later photograph.

*T*he chancel and east window of St Michael's parish church, 1923 and 2005. The earlier photograph records the interior before it was rebuilt following a fire in 1994. Virtually everything within the chancel of the ancient church was lost. This included a nineteenth-century stained-glass window dedicated to the memory of successful shipbuilder Isaac Scott and his family and a carved Caen stone and marble pulpit, erected to the memory of Miss Mary Dickinson. The later photograph shows the interior of the rebuilt church. It is very much plainer than the earlier gothic-style church it replaced. Much of its design actually reflects more of the Georgian features of an earlier church destroyed in another fire, particularly the plain, circular columns rising through the galleries to support the roof. As the congregation of St Michaels has greatly diminished over the last few decades, much of the renovated church has now been converted into meeting rooms for the local community.

*T*he former Presbyterian church, now the Workington Christian Fellowship Church, *c.* 1979 and 2005. The earlier photograph shows the former Presbyterian church which stood in Sanderson Street. It was demolished to make way for the recent town centre redevelopment and its site is now within the Debenhams store. Completed in 1889, the English gothic-style church had a neat, well-balanced façade of red sandstone and coursed ashlar stonework designed by Maryport architect Charles W. Eaglesfield. In 1972, the Presbyterian church merged with the Congregational church to become the United Reform church and the congregation moved to the South William Street church. The vacant church was later acquired by the Workington Christian Fellowship or Pentecostal Church. The later photograph shows the new Pentecostal church just off Central Square, beneath the parapet walls of the Oxford Street bridge. This site was formerly occupied by the goods shed of the Cleator & Workington Junction Railway.

*L*ooking west down the south side of Guard Street, *c.* 1972 and 2006. The earlier illustration is a sketch recording the front elevation of Workington's first secondary school. The central section of this school building is the oldest and was first built in 1831, having been endowed by Thomas Wilson. In Victorian times the school accommodated

around 500 older scholars, who were educated up to the then statutory school leaving age of fourteen. Some pupils stayed on until sixteen to take the equivalent of the school certificate examinations. Extended in 1882 and 1899, Guard Street school became the town's new grammar or higher grade school in 1902. After the grammar school later relocated to the same site as the technical college in Park Lane, Guard Street became known as Central School and remained a secondary school. In February 1951, it was renamed Wilson Secondary Modern School after its founder some 120 years earlier. Wilson School closed after Moorclose School (now Southfield) was built in 1967. It was subsequently demolished in the early 1980s and office premises now occupy the site.

Workington College, *c.* 1938 and Workington Community Hospital, 2005, both viewed from the south-west. The earlier photograph shows the attractive red-brick building, completed in 1912, which occupied this Park Lane site. The college changed its name several times over the years; up until 1929 it was known as Workington County Technical College and Secondary School. Prior to 1945, it became the West Cumberland Secondary School and Cumberland Technical College. Thereafter, it was known as Workington Grammar School and Secondary Technical College, until the new grammar school opened at Stainburn in 1954. Later, the Park Lane premises housed the West Cumbria College, until it moved to the new Lakes College at Lillyhall. Initially the college was quite small with only twelve classrooms accommodating 300 pupils. But it

was considerably extended in 1933-34 with additional workshops, classrooms, laboratories and a mining school (funded by the Miner's Welfare Fund).

*L*ooking west across Vulcans park, *c.* 1965 and 2005. The earlier photograph shows the 1960s style, eight-storey Technical College which dominated the town's skyline for almost forty years. It was demolished in 2000, along with the remainder of the older college buildings which extended through to Park Lane, to make way for a new community hospital. Workington Technical College was first built in 1912 on the opposite side of the park. It later merged with Whitehaven college to become West Cumbria College. When the new college was built at Distington, on the site of the former Lillyhall School, West Cumbria College moved there. The later photograph shows the same view across Vulcans park towards the rear of the hospital

that replaced the college. Vulcans park was laid out between 1928-30 and was once the focal point for the leisure time of the townspeople.

Other local titles published by Tempus

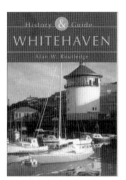

Workington
RICHARD L.M. BYERS

Using a fascinating sequence of old photographs this book traces some of the many developments that have taken place in Workington over the last century. The images highlight the importance of local industry in the town, including coal mining and shipbuilding, which employed generations of townspeople. Later, in Victorian times, the town became a major centre for the production of iron and steel and as a result saw further dramatic growth in size and importance.

0 7524 3295 8

Whitehaven History & Guide
ALAN W. ROUTLEDGE

This history of Whitehaven tells the story of the town from the time of its first Roman fort to the present day. Mining was once so intensive here that 3,800 workers raised 232 tons of coal per man per year, and the harbour was at one time the most important in the country after London. As well as an in-depth history of the area, its people and its industrial past, the book explores local landmarks of Whitehaven and includes a guided tour enabling the reader to embark on a tour of the fascinating harbour area, to explore the Beacon, the Quays and the Marina.

0 7524 2602 8

Maryport
KEITH THOMPSON

This important collection old photographs shows some of the changes seen in the town over the last century and a half. The images show the town's industry and the everyday life and times of local people throughout the period. It will be a nostalgic tour for those who remember the old days and a revelation for those who are new to the area or are too young to remember them.

0 7524 2158 1

Workington Association Football Club
PAUL EADE

This book of over 200 images charts the progress and successes of the club from the early days in the North Eastern League to entry into the Football League in 1951, the twenty-six years spent there, and the Reds' fortunes since their return to non-League football in 1977. Particular tribute is paid to the Football League period, including Bill Shankly's period as Workington manager from 1954 to 1955 and the classic FA Cup tie at Borough Park in January 1958 when the Reds hosted Manchester United in front of a record 21,000-strong crowd.

0 7524 2818 7

If you are interested in purchasing other books published by Tempus, or in case you have difficulty finding any Tempus books in your local bookshop, you can also place orders directly through our website

www.tempus-publishing.com